WYMONDHAM

Step back into the past and enjoy th

Visitors to the town often wonder about the origi
pronounced *Wind-um* in Norfolk. Opinions v
place-name ending *ham* can mean a village or
Saxon times. Many of these developed into small
The Saxon *wynn* or *win* means a pleasant place and ount.
This suggests that *win-munte-ham* meant the village o or slope.
If you stand by the Market Cross and look down the n you can see you
are at the top of a slope; when you walk up Market Stre wards the Cross you
are going up a hill.

EARLY SETTLEMENT

Less than a mile from the Market Place, an excavation took place in 2005 at a site on Browick Road, prior to a possible development there. The site lies in a valley and is bisected by a drainage ditch and hedgerow. The ditch was part of a system which drained into the River Tiffey. At the northern end of the site is the oval ring work known as Moot, or Mote Hill.

It is part of a rich archaeological landscape which had been occupied and farmed from the New Stone Age, 3,600 BC. Items which had been found nearby, prior to the 2005 excavation, included a Bronze Age sword, Iron Age Iceni coins, 16 Roman coins, a bracelet, ring and brooch together with an early Saxon brooch.

View of the excavation site from Browick Road with Moot Hill in the background.

Beneath the field in the foreground of the mysterious Moot Hill, evidence of some of the earliest settlers in Wymondham was found. From New Stone Age times, 3,600–3,000 BC, pits and ditches were revealed and a probable water course, from which pottery and worked flint were recovered.

Items from the Bronze Age, 3,000–1,800 BC, include a pot boiler mound. Pot boilers were flints heated in a fire then placed in a cooking pot to heat the contents, because the pot could not withstand the heat of the fire. From the mid Bronze Age period, pottery and worked flint were found.

Dated to 300–100 BC in the Iron Age, ditches, post holes, pits, pottery and organic remains, which included oat, barley and wheat, were found. Also a partially exposed roundhouse structure was revealed in one of the trenches.

Evidence from the Romano British period, 43 BC–410 AD, included ditches, pits, a probable aisled timber-built structure, a coin and some decorated pottery.

From early to mid Saxon times, 410–650 AD, a hearth or oven was revealed, some mid Saxon pottery and, near the hearth, the remains of what is thought to have been a sunken featured building.

Other organic remains recovered from the site include bones of red deer, pig, boar and cattle.

Saxon cemeteries have often been found along river valleys. It is believed that there is a cemetery south of Browick Road sloping towards the Tiffey, where a 6th century East Anglian brooch was found.

It is likely that the early settlers may have later moved from Browick to a more favoured location in the parish, the Wymondham we know today.

Wymondham is the second largest parish in Norfolk and touches on 19 other parishes. In one of these, **Crownthorpe,** very near to the Wymondham parish boundary, remarkable evidence was discovered in 1982 from the Romano British period.

Crownthorpe was on a Roman road between Caistor St Edmund and Denver in West Norfolk. On Roman roads there was a settlement every 10–15 km, a day's march. Crownthorpe was probably an overnight stopping place with a bath house, inn, shops and a market where locals would sell their produce. Buildings were made of timber, wattle and daub. The heyday of this settlement was c.10–60 AD, dated by coins discovered there.

A very special hoard found there was of Iron Age and Roman drinking vessels now held by Norwich Castle Museum. The objects include cups that display a fusion of Celtic and Roman styles. They were possibly a wine set consisting of seven bronze drinking vessels, from the mid 1st century AD. The strainer with its lion's head has been crudely repaired. The patera and saucepan came from South Italy, but the two unique duck cups were locally made.

There is evidence for concentrated areas of bronze working here and possibly enamelling. A collection of over 100 brooches have been found which were manufactured locally and 25 military items have also been discovered.

There is also evidence for Bronze Age, Early and Late Saxon, Medieval and early Post Medieval activity in the area. The damaged foundations of a Roman-Celtic temple c.100–200 AD have been partly excavated. It was some 72 square metres in area, constructed of mortared flint with a tiled floor, roof and veranda.

The duck handle of a unique bronze cup.

During the uncertainty after

Cast handle of the patera or shallow bowl.

A handled pan.

the Romans left in 410 AD, the early Saxon kingdoms gradually developed. It is believed that Wymondham, a Saxon estate, may have become an ecclesiastical unit with a minster.

In 867 AD the Danes began to invade and plunder. Then in 869 a Viking army wintered at Thetford and the Danes began to settle in East Anglia. Despite Alfred the Great's efforts, the Danes did not submit until 917 during the reign of Edward the Elder. The Wymondham street names Damgate, Churchgate and Flassegate could indicate Danish connections but only one piece of Danish pottery has been found, outside the Abbey wall and part of a decorated spoon north of Tuttles Lane.

However in 1958 a remarkable discovery was found right on the modern parish boundary of **Morley St Peter** and Wymondham.

It was Saxon treasure of 883 silver coins buried in a Thetford ware urn and was the largest and most complete coin hoard of its type. The overwhelming majority of the coins were struck almost certainly in Norwich after 917 AD when Edward the Elder was king and, if so, would seem to confirm that he had established his control and the Danes had left.

Why were the coins hidden here? The old track from Norwich to Thetford may have run nearby and it has been suggested that the coins were stolen from a baggage train being transported, then buried for later recovery. However there are signs of habitation near the site where the coins were found, including animal bones and 50 pieces of late Saxon pottery. Alternatively, could the coins have been the property of one rich person?

Incidentally, the coins were declared Treasure Trove and the payment to the finders was the biggest ever awarded at the time.

BEFORE THE ABBEY

An archaeological evaluation took place prior to the Appeal which resulted in the beautiful extension to Wymondham Abbey. This tells the story of the church past and present.

The excavation revealed the foundations of a church before the Abbey which sealed a burial. This may mean there was an even earlier church nearby. Other artefacts could possibly indicate activity dating to Roman and Saxon times. Butchered animal bones may relate to a manorial complex on the site.

In Domesday Book 1086, 327 people are mentioned as landowners giving a possible population of about 1500. Stigand, Bishop of N. Elmham Norfolk, then Winchester and finally Archbishop of Canterbury, held Wymondham in 1066. It passed to Earl Ralf, Earl of East Anglia, from whom it was confiscated when he rebelled against William the Conqueror in 1075. It then reverted to the Crown.

WILLIAM D'ALBINI

The early development of Wymondham was closely linked with the fortunes of William d'Albini I, a trusted supporter of William Rufus 1087–1100. D'Albini was a loyal servant to his successor Henry I 1100–35 and was appointed *pincerna regis*, royal butler. This office passed down through his descendants to the Dukes of Norfolk. He was also granted part of the royal demesne lands–the honour of Buckenham, Kenninghall, Fersfield and the manor of Wymondham.

The founding of Wymondham Priory

The year 1107 marked two great events in d'Albini's life, his marriage to Maud Bigod and the founding of a Benedictine priory as a daughter house of St Albans Abbey at Wymondham. The monks would pray for the souls of the founder, wife and children and the priory would be a symbol of his wealth and power.

The Priory was a high status stone building, visible for miles, underlining d'Albini's political power, wealth and prestige; a permanent reminder of Norman dominance.

D'Albini intended the building should be used by the Prior and 12 monks and also by the townspeople as their Parish church. But no clear directions were given as to who had jurisdiction in which part of the church, a recipe for future trouble which lasted for several centuries.

He endowed the Priory with his manor house, courtyard, orchards, fisheries and mill and other rights to revenues. The monks could hold a three day fair on the anniversary of the birth of the Virgin Mary. They probably lived in d'Albini's manor house until the monastic buildings were complete c.1130, when the first prior was appointed.

The founding of the priory was a turning point in the history of Wymondham which was gradually transformed from a small Saxon settlement into a busy Norman town. D'Albini's wife Maud died soon after 1120. William continued to serve King Stephen 1135–1154 and died in 1139.

On 23 December 1833 we get a possible glimpse into the world of the d'Albinis. Workmen were clearing part of the abbey ruins when they came upon two lead coffins, one about six feet by one foot and another one foot by half a foot.

Artist's impression based on the original plan of the 1834 excavation.

The body in the largest coffin was bound like an Egyptian mummy. A mass of auburn hair was around the neck. The smaller coffin contained the body of an unborn child and cumin seed. It is believed that the larger coffin was that of Maud, d'Albini's wife, and the smaller one that of his unborn child. The smaller coffin was exhibited in 1847 and it will form part of the new medieval gallery at

Norwich Castle Museum.

Stone coffins with the remains of two monks with remnants of woollen cloth were found at the entrance of the chapter house. These were dated prior to 1300. Seeds of valerian rubra, *all heal*, from the coffins, were grown and exhibited in 1836. These coffins remain at Wymondham Abbey

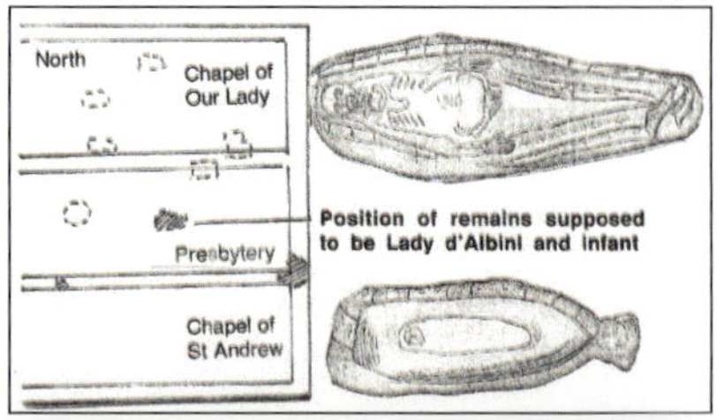

Upper: plan showing positions of coffins. Lower: valerian rubra, seeds of which were found in the coffins.

MOOT OR MOTE HILL

This earthwork is next to an ancient landscape which has been cultivated and occupied since 3,000 BC. It is located on the edge of the Hart's Farm estate and Kett's Park. There is no public access to the site. A mile and a half from the centre of Wymondham, it is isolated and forgotten by the modern world, but retains an air of mystery and may have had special significance in early times.

Moot Hill is an oval-shaped structure, with a ditch, rampart and central enclosure. It is just over four acres in area. Its south eastern side was partly destroyed when the railway was built in 1845.

What was Moot Hill? A ringwork of possibly 12th century date, but was the site originally a Saxon moot or meeting place?

The latest thinking is that it was built by the d'Albinis but was short-lived because they preferred to live at Buckenham. A castle at Old Buckenham dates from 1106 but a second one was built at New Buckenham c. 1145 by another d'Albini. This can be visited. A new Norman town developed there.

Remains of rampart and ditch.

Although there has been no systematic excavation there, the following finds have been recorded:

1930 – Mr Batterley found a pot boiler. A Bronze Age pot boiler mound was discovered during the recent dig in the adjacent fields. Animal bones were also found.

1980 – a small excavation by Mr Rose found a gold ring dated 1306 belonging to Katherine Bigod, a descendant of Roger Bigod, who was a large landowner listed in Domesday. She was married to Roger Fitz-Ortet who held Stanfield Manor at that time.

BECKET'S CHAPEL

Standing at the junction of Church and Middleton Streets, it was founded by William d'Albini III c.1174. It was dedicated to St Thomas à Becket, the murdered Archbishop of Canterbury. It became the chapel of St Thomas's religious gild. After the dissolution of Wymondham Abbey in 1538, and the abolition of religious gilds in 1547, it became the town's grammar school.

Becket's Chapel c. 1850.

If you walk along Middleton Street you will see the grammar school crest over three buildings on the left (see page 8).

Becket's Chapel has been much altered and used by the community as a public hall and town library. It is now a wonderful setting for an Arts Centre. All are welcome to enjoy the frequently changing exhibitions.

THE MARKET

In 1135 a charter for a three day annual fair in September was issued to the monks of Wymondham by King Stephen. This was renewed by Henry II.

About 1180 William d'Albini III described Becket's Chapel as '*standing in my market place surrounded by a hedge*'. There is evidence for a market place with Church Street, the Abbey churchyard, Vicar Street and Middleton Street as its boundaries.

Top left: Becket's Chapel. Top right: school laboratory. Bottom left: York House, former boarding house. Bottom right: The Priory, the main school building from 1835.

The eastern gate to the churchyard was called the Marketstead gate. In 1204 King John granted a charter to William d'Albini for a fair in September and another charter to him for a market on Fridays, changed to Tuesdays in 1207.

In early medieval times markets were held in churchyards on Sundays. The Papacy opposed the connection between parish churches and trading and, in 1285, Edward I declared that neither fairs nor markets were to be held in churchyards.

The present market place

In the 1100s another market could have developed on or near its present site. One of Wymondham's manors Grisaugh, controlled the market here until the 20th century.

The first market crosses were shafted and had stepped stone bases. These gradually developed into covered crosses and Wymondham's first may have been an open rectangular market hall with a room above. In 1615, on 11 June, it was destroyed by the Great Fire. The present octagonal cross was built 1617–18 costing £25 17s which was loaned by a leading townsman Philip Culyer.

The agents of the lord of the manor wanted to build shops around it but the townspeople objected and won. The Cross is now owned by the town council and makes a wonderful tourist information point.

A carving on the Market Cross.

There is still a Friday market and a farmer's market on the 3rd Saturday of each month.

THE GAME PLACE AND KETT'S REBELLION

The Watch and Play Society produced the Wymondham Play or *Wymondhamgame*. The Kett family were closely linked to this event at the Game Place which was at or near the Bridewell. The '*Wymondhamgame*' hit the headlines in 1549, the year of Kett's Rebellion, when it took place on the weekend of the 6/7 July.

The story of what happened next has been told many times. Members of the audience and those present for the Wymondham Fair discussed the injustice of fencing off the common land from the poor. Groups went to Morley to pull down the fences of Master Hobart there and of John Flowerdew of Hethersett. But Flowerdew paid the rioters to pull down Kett's fences instead, which resulted in Kett becoming the leader of a protest march to Norwich. Many joined this march and camped on Mousehold Heath. This protest against the local gentry developed into a conflict with the Crown. It ended in tears with the 3,000 rebels killed and the hanging of Robert Kett at Norwich Castle and his brother William from the west tower of Wymondham Abbey.

What began at the Game Place also led to a government ban on the performance of '*all plays, interludes and dialogues in English*' from 9 August to 1 November 1549, throughout the kingdom. In the 1550s plays about religion or the governance of

Scene from a re-enactment of Kett's Rebellion in 1999, for the 450th anniversary of the rebellion.

the state were also banned.

THE BRIDEWELL

In the 16th century Poor Law Acts ordered JPs to set up Houses of Correction or Bridewells to punish those who would not work in return for help from the parish. The earliest mention of a Wymondham Bridewell is 1619.

By the 1770s it was so badly run that John Howard, the prison reformer, when he visited in 1779, called it one of the 'vilest prisons in England'. His verdict led to local JPs headed by Sir Thomas Beevor creating a 'new model' prison with individual cells in 1785. When the prison closed in 1878 the Bridewell was used as the police station and later a magistrate's court.

Beautifully kept and run entirely by volunteers, part of the building is now used as a museum. As the 'memory of the town', it has displays about brush making, farming, pubs and the Bridewell's uses over the past 300 years. There are also two new recreated former shops. There is also a unique and colourful display about Kett's Rebellion.

A display about Stanfield Hall reveals more about its links with Amy Robsart and Lord Robert Dudley, favourite of Elizabeth I. The hall was later the scene of the notorious Rush murders which aroused great national interest in the 1840s.

The museum tea room created from the original exercise yard of the police station, serves drinks, homemade cakes and snacks.

THE CIVIL WAR

In the early 17th century Puritanism, a movement to purify and reform the church which included the abolition of bishops, was growing. The strength of this religious nonconformity in Wymondham meant it was more likely to support Parliament. Sir John Hobart, lord of the manor, a firm Puritan was a leading member of the Eastern Association, an army recruited from the eastern counties, which later became an important part of the parliamentary forces. Another local figure who was a member of that Association was Martin Sedley of Morley. Sir Thomas Wodehouse of nearby Kimberley Hall also supported Parliament.

There were few military events in the town. In 1643 200 people from Norwich

Original pottery flat back models of Stanfield Hall & Potash Farm, home of the murderer Rush, produced for sale.

came almost as far as Wymondham to meet the Earl of Manchester and Colonel Cromwell, Parliamentary officers. Later, 500 soldiers following the Earl of Manchester stopped in Wymondham and pulled down the organ in the church, before moving on to Norwich. This incident typifies Puritan attacks on the Church of England at the time.

As the war progressed, the town authorities and churchwardens had a duty to help the wounded who came to Wymondham or through it. One was John Bunn who was paid 3 shillings a week for 7 weeks and 2 shillings for 15 weeks. Those who were sent to war had to be provided with clothing, for example, three knapsacks for the soldiers with a Captain Harvey.

The Town Book records that 121 people maimed by the war were helped with payments while recovering from wounds in the town before going home. Support was given to 15 widows and children of men who were killed in the war. £43 2s 9d was paid in compensating wounded soldiers, in some cases providing financial support for up to five weeks. One touching entry reads *'paid for a sheet for a poor soldier who died homeward as he came through the town'*.

The only Civil War soldier from Wymondham, whose will has been found, was Robert Wildman. He was a Roundhead in Cromwell's army and served Parliament for ten years, fighting at the decisive battle of Naseby 1645, which led to the King's downfall. Money from the sale of his pistol, saddle and bridle went to his widow and children.

WYMONDHAM CHURCHES

In 1633 Archbishop Laud was determined to purge the Church of England of Puritans. Wren, Bishop of Norwich, was an ardent supporter and his religious persecution led to 134 people, who refused to conform to the doctrine and practice of the Church of England, fleeing from the area around Wymondham. James Gedney and Stephen and Thomas Gooch went to Rotterdam where they founded an English church.

The Fairland Church

One of the Puritan complaints was lack of preaching so 'lecturers' were appointed to fill this gap. In 1644 Wymondham authorities made an agreement with John Money to be the lecturer. Two years later a group were keen to form a Congregational or Independent church in Wymondham; in such churches power is invested in the congregation not bishops. By 1652 there was a Congregational Church in Wymondham involving John Money, which later developed into the United Reformed Church.

Fairland United Reformed Churtch today.

After Charles II was restored in 1660 his parliament passed the Act of Uniformity to enforce a revised Book of Common Prayer and all ministers had to comply. However eventually Charles issued licences for Puritan meetings to be held in private houses addressed by specific persons.

John Money who seems to have been the parish minister at the Abbey Church for a time was ejected in 1664. He then took out a licence to preach and there were four houses in the town where Puritan meetings took place.

The present Fairland Church building was put up by Roger Gay in 1715 but was less than half the size of the present one which was enlarged in 1876.

Today the Fairland Church Centre plays an important part in community life hosting meetings of various clubs and organisations. Notably it serves as a meeting place for the Pabulum Cafe for people with dementia and their carers. They have their own garden there.

Baptist Church

This church began in Friarscroft in 1796 moving to Queen Street in 1797. This building is the present school room which had a baptistery pool under the floor. The local doctor's daughter recalled that this church would borrow their water cart to get water from the River Tiffey for baptisms. In the 1940s pupils of Lyndhurst School, which used the school room, remember the pool as an unusual air raid shelter.

The church was damaged by incendiary bombs during the war. The foundation stone of the present church, which seats 300, was laid in 1909. Bricks were sold at 5/- each and there are some initialled ones on the south side. The church runs the Roots Community Café and hosts the Norwich Food Bank at Wymondham.

Roman Catholic Church

In the early days, Roman Catholics met in a chapel behind 18–20 Cock Street. In 1937 the Elms site in Norwich Road was bought by the church. After Father Cowin became priest at the end of the war, a national appeal was launched in 1948 to create a permanent memorial for those who lost their lives as prisoners of war in the Far East. This enabled a church designed by Dominic Purcel to be built. The church was extended in 2001 based on a design by Paul Lucas; it was awarded the South Norfolk Design Award.

The church's parish hall is the meeting place for the Wymondham Community Fridge and Café which uses food near its sell buy date to provide a meal once a week – it is open to all.

Methodist Church

Primitive Methodists worshipped in Norwich Road from 1844, moving to Back Lane in 1855. The chapel became too small and the trustees found a new site at Cornelius Tipple's old warehouse in Town Green. They paid £300 for the site and Edward Boardman, a Norwich architect, designed a church for 500 people in 1871.

Today the Town Green Centre attached to the church is used for community activities and as a Day Centre.

The Religious Society of Friends or Quakers

This group of Dissenters was founded in the 17th century by George Fox. Its members believed they should look within themselves to lead the true Christian life. In 1654 one of his followers, Richard Hubberthorne, spoke about his faith in the Abbey Church. This offended the minister and the local JP who sent him to Wymondham Bridewell from where he was later transferred to Norwich Castle prison. George White, another Quaker, also came to the town and converted several people, including John Lawrence, a doctor and captain in the Parliamentary army. When Fox spoke at Lawrence's house in Wramplingham, it was said that as many as 1,000 attended.

Quaker numbers grew in Wymondham and meetings were held in private houses and later in an old chapel on the Chapel Lane Bridge. In 1687 their own meeting house was built nearby. The Quakers were persecuted after Cromwell's fall and until the Toleration Act of 1689. Support gradually declined and the meeting house closed in 1950. Happily woodwork, tiles and furniture were sent to America and incorporated in the Quaker Earlham College. A small group of Quakers still meet in Wymondham.

ROADS AND RAILWAYS

The road from Norwich to London marked on Gough's 14th century map passed through Wymondham and Attleborough. The terrain between the towns was marshy and difficult for travellers and trade. Originally, parishes were responsible for its upkeep but more needed to be done.

Eventually a Turnpike Trust was set up for this road in 1695. It was the first in Norfolk and the second in the country. The Trust established a body to collect road tolls to repair this highway.

The road pillar in remembrance of Sir Edwin Rich.

But the road was repaired 20 years before the Turnpike Act and a pillar was erected '*in gratefull remembrance of Sir Edwin Rich Knt. who freely gave ye sume of two hundred pounds towards ye repaire of ye Highway between Wymondham & Attleborough AD 1675*'.

The pillar is believed to have originally been a sun dial which stood on the north side of the old A11 near Dial Farm. It is now located in a lay-by on the B1172 next to a small roundabout.

During her journey through England in 1698, Celia Fiennes passed through Wymondham. She described it as, '*a little market town mostly on a causey....the road was secured by a barr at which passengers pay a penny a horse in order to the mending of the way*'.

The turnpike roads led to a demand for regular reliable transport and ushered in the 'golden age' of the stage coach 1780s-1830s. More inns were needed and trades associated with coaching, like harness makers, blacksmiths and wheelwrights. By the 1830s three coaches ran daily between London and Norwich calling at the Griffin, White Hart or King's Head in Wymondham.

THE RAILWAY STATION

Wymondham railway station opened in July 1845 as a stopping point on the line between Norwich and Brandon, providing a link to London via Ely. By 1846 a link to Yarmouth was complete and daily excursions costing 3d (1p) were available; trips to London cost 1s 6d. A branch line from Wymondham to East Dereham and Fakenham was opened in 1849, extending to Wells.

A branch line to Forncett was completed by 1881. This allowed the passengers from North Norfolk to avoid Norwich by changing at Wymondham and catching the London train at Forncett station. A truly local line it even carried medicines for patients in villages along the line. It closed in 1939 but was used to store explosives wagons where the banks were high. You can walk along the former railway track which is part of the Tiffey Trails Lizard Walk.

Railways were a body blow to road transport and the stage coaches. But the King's Head Inn continued to flourish and provided horse drawn cabs to meet each train. Rail transport also affected the town's market which was never quite so successful again. The East Dereham line closed to passengers in 1969. It has been reopened by the Mid Norfolk Railway Preservation Trust. The 15 mile preserved standard gauge railway can be boarded at the Abbey Halt in Becketswell Road. From here you travel through country stations and at certain times of the year steam trains are used. Wildlife is abundant during the journey.

The railway carriage tea room at Wymondham station.

Wymondham station was restored by David Turner who ran a 'Brief Encounter' Tea Room. The popular bistro retains its railway carriage-style tea room.

BREWING IN WYMONDHAM

Wealthy families such as the Randalls and the Burroughs were the main brewers in the 18th century. However, by the 1780s the brewery owned by John Stephenson Cann was the foremost in the town and also important in Norfolk. This brewery occupied a large block of property between Queen Street and the

Forecourt of station in 1908, with horse drawn cabs waiting to take rail passengers to the King's Head.

Near right: the former brewery buildings about 1900.

Town House Hotel in Market Street, which backed on to Brewery Lane. In 1824 Cann joined with Clarke; they later purchased another Wymondham brewery, Harveys. Cann and Clarke's brewery was eventually sold to Morgans of Norwich in 1894, bringing brewing in the town to an end.

Before being pulled down in the 1960s and the new shops were built, the brewery buildings were used by SD Page brush maker for cleaning and dyeing brush fibres. In 1931 William Smith opened a swimming pool in one of the former beer vats; it lasted until 1953. It was the only one in Wymondham until the Leisure Centre was opened.

Wymondham's pubs

Of the original 30 or so, six remain. All offer a warm welcome in attractive and historic settings.

Green Dragon: This Tudor alehouse had been extended and altered from the mid 15th century. Earlier called the 'shoppes' it is believed the front arched windows were formerly shops. Stories

A carving on the façade of the Green Dragon.

about a possible secret tunnel between the Dragon and the Abbey have a more mundane explanation. The creation of a new surface water system in 1980 revealed brick sewers at the south end of Church Street about a metre high and 1.5 metres wide. As the tunnels proceed along Church Street, they become oval in shape. A similar system exists in Lavenham, Suffolk.

The Queen's Head.

Cross Keys: dates from the 16th century at least. The right side of the façade was a shop which was incorporated into the pub in 1965. Its mock Tudor frontage matches the original timber frame.

White Hart: behind its Georgian façade lies a building called the Hart mentioned in a 1525 document. A former coaching inn, an excavation of the coach entrance, on the left side of the façade, showed it was always part of the original building leading to Wellgate which connects with Back Lane.

Queen's Head: the flint cellar maybe what remains of the pre-1615 fire building.

The Railway: originally named the Dun Cow changed its name after the railway station opened in 1845 initially to the Railway Commercial Hotel.

The Feathers in Town Green.

The Feathers: dates from the 18th century or earlier. It has been known as the Three Feathers and the Prince of Wales Feathers.

The Robert Kett: this newer pub is named after the leader of the Norfolk Rebellion. It is an integral part of a residential estate built during the expansion of the town.

WEAVING

In the Middle Ages, wool was the 'golden fleece' of the economy. In Tudor times enclosure for sheep farming became very popular with landowners. In this area the issue was one of the causes of discontent which led to Kett's Rebellion in 1549. Wymondham was involved in all aspects of the textile trade and woollen cloth was produced here from the 1500s. Linen weaving was also important and there were wealthy chapmen or travelling salesmen in wool in the town. One, Richard Lincoln had this timber-framed house built in Bridewell Street in 1616.

Richard Lincoln's house built in 1616.

Weaving flourished between the 1740s and 1830s. In 1747 the vicar counted 155 weavers in Wymondham. White's Directory 1836 recorded 600 as the number of looms in the town. For a time more people were employed in weaving than any other industry. The noise of the 'clacking' looms must have echoed through the town. The number of weavers had fallen to 60 in 1845 but Wymondham weavers then switched to other fabrics, particularly bombazine, a mixture of silk and worsted. This was made into a dress material which was often dyed black and used for mourning clothes. The only other places this fabric was made were in Norwich and Kidderminster.

The 1841 census listed over 70 weavers in the town. But, because the weavers had switched to making new fabrics, their numbers had risen to over 320 by 1851.

Weavers' houses in Chain Entry.

During the 'golden age' of weaving in the 19th century there were three weaving factories - in Damgate, Town Green and Friarscroft. But the Industrial Revolution, with its steam powered machinery and factory production in northern England, spelt ruin for Wymondham weavers and all the factories were closed by the early 20th century.

If you walk down Chain Entry, accessible from the car park in Market Street, note the tall houses on the left of the alleyway used by weavers. Miss Lowe, born 1893 in the doctor's house, now Town House Hotel, remembered seeing a woman weaving in one of these houses from her bedroom window at the back.

BRUSH MAKING

Wymondham has been known for its wood turners from Tudor times and the nearby hamlet of Spooner Row must have got its name from spoon making carried on there. A 'spoon of Wymondham' appeared in wills, a sign of the esteem in which they were held. Spoons and spigots are carved on the Market Cross beams and appear on the town sign.

In the early 19th century Robert Semmence started in a small way on a treadle lathe as a wood turner. By the 1830s he was producing small wooden domestic tableware. When demand for this fell he made brush backs for SD Page of Norwich. Page's set up a factory in Lady's Lane, Wymondham in 1888 to make their own brush backs. By 1901 machinery was well established in the brush works on Lady's Lane and a key element in the Page business. In World War One four million brushes were made for the armed forces. In 1922 Page's joined with D Mathew to form the Briton Brush company and by the mid-1920s its products were known world wide.

Two of the company's successful slogans were 'Briton Brush sweeps the

Some Briton Brush workers.

A works outing for Briton Brush workers.

world' and 'a Briton brush for every use' ; in fact 2,000 different types of brush were produced there. During these years over 600 were employed in the factory. Machines like the Gane filling machine which fixed tufts into the brush stocks at the rate of 50 knots a minute revolutionised brush making. It became the most up to date factory; brush making put Wymondham on the country's industrial map.

A unique exhibition which includes a Gane machine used by Briton Brush, can be seen at Wymondham Heritage Museum.

In 1917 the Co-operative Wholesale Society Brush Company bought the Chapel Lane sawmills of George Semmence and set up a steam powered factory there in 1922. It employed some 200 workers and by 1932 was producing 'good brushes for the millions' as well as non brush products like the Samson non slip deck chair. Its landmark chimney was demolished by controlled explosion in 1988.

There were also several small brush makers working from home who produced specialised brushes. For decades brush making was inseparably linked with Wymondham.

WORLD WAR ONE

The war memorial stands at the junction of Vicar Street and Middleton Street. There are 143 men listed and most are buried in the major cemeteries in Europe and the Middle East; there are nine graves in Wymondham cemetery. 750 volunteered and 450 joined up in 1916. Brief stories of some of the fallen remind us of the impact on families and the town.

Three of the Kerridge brothers were killed and a fourth was injured. He was able to carry on the butchers shop in Market Street, now Wymondham Motorist Centre. Company Quarter Master Sgt JB Cross contracted enteric fever in Gallipoli and died in hospital in Malta where he is buried. Dr Hughes, a local GP, was killed in the Dardanelles and lies in the 7th Field Ambulance cemetery.

Harry Daniels wearing his Victoria Cross.

There was a Red Cross Hospital in the Vicarage Room and Abbotsford where 78 local nurses cared for over 800 patients in all.

CSM Harry Daniels VC MC was born in the town. He earned his VC at Neuve Chapelle in 1915 when, under heavy machine gun fire, he cut the wire impeding the advance of his men. By the memorial, is the special stone presented to towns where a VC winner was born. There is also an information board at the memorial about his colourful life and a commemorative seat.

Staff and patients at the Red Cross hospital at Abbotsford.

WORLD WAR TWO

Eric Standley, one of the first ARP volunteers

The war memorial lists 45 people who died during the war, including three civilians. Two of these died on air bases and the Earl of Kimberley, who had left his peaceful estate for London, was killed during an air raid the night he arrived there.

While the war raged throughout the world, the townsfolk were fully engaged at home in the 'people's war'. There was big campaign to involve them in a voluntary capacity in many different activities – such as Air Raid Wardens, Fire Watchers and Home Guard.

The first challenge of the volunteers and many householders was to receive, house and care for, over 1,000 evacuees from Gravesend. Their efforts were much appreciated by the newcomers. Later in the war evacuees from Norwich and Walthamstow arrived.

The American Army Hospital at Morley.

Other new faces in town included many American servicemen. Hethel air base and the American Army Hospital at Morley were the nearest. After the D Day landings and the Normandy campaign that followed, over 3,250 wounded Americans arrived in hospital trains at Wymondham station and were then taken in ambulances to Morley.

The chairman of the Urban District Council, Edwin Gooch, led the council and the many volunteers in organising the defence of the town and many other tasks. His wife Ethel, a town councillor, founded the Wymondham branch of the Women's Voluntary Service and liaised with the Women's Institute and other local groups working to support

Edwin and Ethel Gooch in 1951.

townspeople and the evacuees. In 1951 she became the first woman chair of the council.

Edwin, 1889–1964, son of a blacksmith in Fairland Street, was President of the National Union of Agricultural Workers 1930–64 promoting the welfare of farm workers. He held the seat of North Norfolk for the Labour Party 1945–63. In 1955 he was elected Chairman of the Labour Party.

At his funeral his niece recalls that along the streets people stood in doorways and men doffed their hats as the cortege passed. Together Edwin and Ethel made a huge contribution to the war effort and the life of the town in general.

There is still an Ex Servicemen's Club in the town at the old Regal Cinema, which hosts the Regal Experience, whose mainly vintage films are much enjoyed by local people and many others.

GREEN SPACES

Sports at King's Head Meadow at the turn of the 20th century.

King's Head Meadow: the former King's Head Inn, now the site of the Co-op supermarket, closed in 1962. It had a meadow in Back Lane, now the home of the town football club. It has had a long association with the Wymondham Sports events 1884–1909, various celebrations and carnivals.

Tiffey Trails: an award winning project launched by the Wymondham Arts Forum in 2004, it aimed to celebrate the valley of the River Tiffey with its green spaces, wildlife and history.

Near the start of the trail is the Lizard; the Lizard Pasture

The viewing platform.

and Oxford Common are public open spaces managed by the Lizard Trustees for the benefit of the townspeople. There is a viewing platform with distant views of the Abbey.

Cemetery Lane viewing platform.

In Cemetery Lane another viewing point overlooks Tolls Meadow, owned by the Council. The River Tiffey flows through the meadow where you can see birds, butterflies and wild flowers; water voles can also be seen. The meadow is managed with the help of volunteers.

Further along the trail by Damgate Bridge there is a riverside walk with lovely views of the Abbey. The popular annual jazz picnic is held in the meadow by the river. At Becketswell Bridge the walk continues to Chapel Bridge; then a footpath continues to the Kimberley Hall estate.

The riverside walk.

The Fairland: an attractive remnant of the old common land on the eastern edge of the town, which originally extended further south.

Kett's Park: the newest green space, on the outskirts of the town – it has football, tennis and other sports facilities and a community hall. The new town council offices nearby and the archive are due to open in 2020.

Priory Gardens: a pleasant area off Middleton Street, with seats, trees and flower beds, was an acre of land where the old grammar school had its gym and fives court.

Browick Road Recreation Ground also has skate boarding facilities.

In 1066 Wymondham's population was about 1500. Over the next 900 years it rose very slowly reaching just over 5,000 by 1939. But since the 1960s there has been a significant increase in size with industrial and residential estates now ringing the old town. At the 2011 census there were 14,400 people. However the enduring appeal of Wymondham's medieval streets at the heart of the town, together with its range of historic buildings–over 220 are listed in the conservation area, still attract many visitors. Many of its wide range of specialist shops are located in historic buildings. The oldest of these is CC Clements in Fairland Street founded in 1875. After a look round the shops there is a good choice of places for coffee, lunch or tea.

This outline of Wymondham's story is for everyone interested in the town, whether townspeople, new residents on the housing estates or visitors from the rest of the country and all over the world. Many of the places and events for us to enjoy are run by volunteers. During a time of rapid change, Wymondham has retained its historic identity and character. Above all it remains a town on a manageable human scale–'*a pleasant place on a hill*'.

SOME FURTHER READING:

Cattermole, P. ed. *Wymondham Abbey,* 2007

Garrard, B. *Wymondham Grammar School,* 2010 WHS

Garner, M. & Wilson, J. ed. *Wymondham, History of a Norfolk Market Town,* 2006 WHS

Hawkins, J. *Wymondham Bridewell,* WHS

Hoare, A.D. *An Unlikely Rebel, Robert Kett & the Norfolk Rising,* 1999 WHS

Hoare, A.D. *On the Trail of Kett's Rebellion in Norfolk 1549: Places people and events,* 2016

Hoare, A.D. & A. *On the Trail of Robert Kett of Wymondham,* 2010 WHS

Hoare, A.D. & A. *When War came to Wymondham 1939–45: what the townspeople experienced, said and did ...,* 2019 Poppyland Publishing

Jary, L.R. *Kett 1549, Rewriting the Rebellion,* 2018 Poppyland Publishing

Miller, M. *Wymondham News from the 1850s,* 2015

Wilson, J. *The Great Fire of Wymondham 1615,* WHS 2013

WHS *The Wymondham Market Cross,* 2018

Yaxley, P. *Wymondham's Old Inns,* 1982 WHS

Yaxley, P. *Around Wymondham in World War Two,* 2010

WHS refers to a Wymondham Heritage Society publication. Many more are available in the Heritage Museum shop.

MAP OF WYMONDHAM

Index